Endorsements for *Ekhō*

From the 'dolomite interior' of Ekhō's cave to Alexa and the 'shadow world' of the internet of things, Roslyn Orlando's wonderful *Ekhō* invents a 'smart speaker' of another kind. When the goods get together 'in bright foreground' to stage a nymphean twelfth night entertainment at a Surrealist party, an if-then reading/writing of 'The self/amplified to itself' disturbs the continuous loop of the poetics of capital. Desire, regret, frivolity, love, ingratitude, ennui, 'noiseless anger'. Repetition, citation, transcription, translation, conjunction, correction, mutation. This serious, playful book has it all!

Kate Lilley

The nymph Ekhō, cursed by the gods and devastated by loss, dissipates into fragments of the voices of others. Now, here, in the reverberating chamber of a hellish present of 'password fatigue' and 'feeble superannuation', Ekhō returns to repeat all that she could not speak before. In this "affair of tongue"—which is also a dialogue of mountains—Roslyn Orlando brilliantly gives a voice to the very personification of no-voice.

Justin Clemens

A wry, dazzling mind-bender. Read immediately.

Chloe Hooper

Ekhō

Roslyn Orlando

Roslyn Orlando is an artist, writer and gardener based in Melbourne on Wurundjeri Country. Her writing and artistic works explore relationships between language, history and technology. She studied Journalism at the University of Sydney, and Arts Politics at Tisch School of the Arts, New York University.

Roslyn Orlando

Ekhō

UPSWELL

First published in Australia in 2024
by Upswell Publishing
Perth, Western Australia
upswellpublishing.com

Upswell operates in the city of Perth, on ancient country of the Whadjuk people of the Noongar nation who remain the spiritual and cultural custodians of this beautiful land. We acknowledge their continuing connection to country and express gratitude to elders past and present for their strength and creativity...Always was, always will be, Aboriginal land.

ISBN: 978-0-6458745-0-1

A catalogue record for this book is available from the National Library of Australia

Cover design by Chil3, Fremantle
Typeset in Foundry Origin by Lasertype
Printed by McPherson's Printing Group

Upswell Publishing is assisted by the State of Western Australia through its funding program for arts and culture.

Camille,

for reading with me.

One thing about hell is the echo is fabulous.

—Anne Carson

PART 1

Prologue

1. Ekhō began with a body
arms, legs, knuckles, trachea
spoke garrulously like a drunk
politician (better intentions
but still) sometimes annoying,
a smile like corn.

2. The other nymphs who hung
out on the sloped mountains of Boeotia
early commune of free love
thought Ekhō benignly entertaining
(she was invited to dinners
but not to séances).

3. Zeus, all puffed up, was not
good at many things except for
getting his way. Hera, his wife,
was even more skilled in this
department. No matter.
On nice days he commonly wanted
to have sex with the mountain nymphs.
He would descend from the heavens
on his gentle winged horse to flirt
and do those other things.
He justified these indiscretions
with a pagan relish for tradition
disguised as morality – a trick taught
to him by mortals.

4. The nymphs were ambivalent
towards his large thunderbolts
but feigned admiration, pleased and
were pleased for a few hours away
from their own daily chores, tending
to the juniper, myrtle, oleander,
cypress.

5. With subscription to
the rumourous wind, Hera,
jealous avenger of infidelity,
came looking.

6. Ekhō with talent for idle chatter
was sent to stall her; to muse
on the price of grain, indulge in
gossip of the local oligarch, angle for
a little more rainfall on the southern
side of the mountain.

7. Hera was first charmed
not like a snake more like
an admirer of emeralds.

8. Found out she had been tricked;
raged predictably cursed
predictably took away
Ekhō's voice so from then on
the nymph could only repeat
the words of others.

9. The shock was all edges.

10. Ekhō, vulnerable now to ill-fate,
fell stiff in love with Narcissus. Repeated
words of his own love to himself, thought maybe
they were getting somewhere.

11. Narcissus just looked at his glassy
reflection in the pond, ancient filter
smoothing out the blemishes,
before drowning himself
down he went cold hard rush
to the bottom.

12. Ekhō despaired, retreated
into the mountains, wasted away.
No arms no legs no trachea,
just echo heard only by those who stop
speaking long enough to listen.

i.

I don't remember myself
when I became a mountain.

I left my body
the way a dream recedes
into light, though some
nymphean convictions
followed me over the threshold
into mountainhood.

There are no photos
(thankfully)
just some scraps of text
degenerating on papyrus.[1]

In terms of my age,
mountains don't measure time
but notice instead
cracks and rivulets
the pressure of wind against
feelings of ingratitude
accumulations and descents.

Even so, the embarrassment
of youth still stings
at the centre of the self;
an eternity of facepalms.
I see him everywhere
and cringe. I see him
in the young mountain
climbers who seek exultant
views; document their

spiritual inclinations with
reaching limbs, screens
predilected to smooth
out the blemishes.

I see him pass along
clifftops unadulterated by
qualm of self; all taught
armour bold conviction
buoyed by a history that
speaks his name over
and over again.

Oh, to give a little push.

ii.

At dawn, visitors
talk in overtones,
fill this thin time
with glottal harmonics.

The wind holds
its breath
root systems quarrel
the soil huddles.
Each day breaks
the back of time's
minor inconsistencies.
Only the shoes
have really changed.

Orthopaedic advancements
offer a more even kilter
less ragged breath less
in tune with the pebbles
and earthly detritus; dark
pockets of the lungs
have fallen into disuse.

deafening chorus
of half-breaths

Bristles of excitable
speech course through
the warm gasp of noon.[2]

Sometimes music pulses,
oil-slicks the air
stains things a grey film
hard to clean off
but not impossible.

On the hour
each hour
8am–6pm
5 days a week
local tour guides
recite my history
with scripted affectation.

It's humiliating
to see oneself summarised
as a quip of one-liners,
as a photo opportunity
at the second lookout.

Amongst the hourly cram
'wows' are sometimes uttered.

Wow wow wow
woooow wow
wowowowowow
wow wow.
It was totally worth it.

iii.

Pictures are geotagged
at the end of each day
to lift the dirt off
the page of the world
and into the resonant
chamber of commerce.
I am located somewhere there:

One hour and a quarter
from Athens / elevation
1,400 metres with
incredible views
to the villas
of Attica / right
after the village,
there is an asphalt
road leading up
to the top / breathtaking /
unbelievable / simply
enchanting / here
is a place to find
yourself and unite with nature /
there are picnic spots
in the fir trees / unfortunately,
on some ridges the human
hand has intervened
with the addition
of wind generators.[3]

I have been described
as an 'amazing mountain',
which I endure.

These days layer themselves
a thick skin of remarks
shifting history like a shoreline
submerging and accreting
the various possibilities
of how things were.

There are certain punctures
I'd like to incise, points
I'd like to correct, wounds
I'd like to open
regarding the sequences
of verbs that constitute
the happenings of my life.

Correction (a)
I am located after Parthenius
and after Virgil, around the time
of Ovid, whence I became somewhat
undisputed in cultural reality,
but before Freud and Lacan,
certainly before Spivak.[4]

I have been triangulated
by these punctures of ego,
spoken for but never to;

re-sounded but never reified,
caught in the crossfire
of the educated guess.

Correction (b)
I had a crush on Hera,
there I said it.

The implications are large,
history is a jumble of losses,
just a few sentences can be inserted
into your edition of *Myths and Legends*,
something like:

'The nymph's self-conscious blathering
led to an illicit affair, an affair of tongue
and touch and figs after which
Zeus' wife was forced to silence the nymph
to mitigate an overuse of thunderbolts
to curse as an act of love.'

Correction (c)
Narcissus came on the scene
(scenes are gatherings of time
demarcated with a backdrop
or by a shadow)
the exemplary rebound
perfect void of intersubjective
projection for my wet sorriness.

Correction (d)
I faintly recall an ambition
to be a lawyer, to relish
in the sanctity of booked words,
to underline sentences,
to point a finger
at the truth of the rain
and to say, 'I object!'
Self-righteous constructs of
justice tend to implode when
you're a mountain.

Even fossils move.

Correction (e)
Mountains have ears just like slugs, bats,
violins, computer screens.

Engines of synthesis.

Sound is absorbed and redistributed
the way onions produce tears the way
love produces bricks, measured via densities
of pleasure that kick at the heart
that roll off the tongue
puffs of
carbon monoxide, invisible but
drastic.

iv.

I endured a lengthy period
of noiseless anger, the kind that
burns the ears, constricts the throat
marks the skin unkindly.

For millennia, I resented
the stiff whistle of stones
dropped off the edges of cliffs
the white noise of the sun
noxious clicking of mantis wings.

I tried to block out the scratching
of history: the creaking of kingdoms,
grinding of blades, jangles of lust,
hollow ringings of ignorance
and even worse, cacophonous
gluttonies of knowledge;
the relentless sandpapering of nature
into the rank and file of civilisation.

And then one day,
a girl no older than
sixteen torrid as the sun
beat herself against me
noise I could not ignore.

She reminded me of a young
nymph named Ekhō, flabbergasted
by the indifferent energies
of a bladed world she burned
like a star out of orbit.

She talked busily with no
poetry no syntax no space
for the nothingness of life
just porous desire, regret,
stretching her heart all over
the place.

I was horrified.

Her busy evocations
annoyed me and yet
all my senses tuned in
hardened up, fell forwards.

v.

The mountains of Boeotia
hold council occasionally
(it's hard to say how often exactly)
to discuss key agenda items
and to assign actions
and to gossip.

ALL:
Mmmmmmmm / mmmmmmmmm
mmmmm / mmmmmmmm
mmmmmmm / mmmmmmm
mmmmmmmmmmmmmmm.

The culture of mountains
has always been networked,
subjective
subjected, we are
negative space carved out
by the conscious substance of the sky.

Council is communicated via
song, as we all know
mountains like to sing
a kind of music that tears through
the forests of history's noise[5];
song with no tradition, as every song
is already being sung so nothing is repeated
just continued.

I have found myself
useful as official scribe,
I make notes and send copies
on the blades of wind turbines.
We are modern like that.

Here are the minutes from Council 20.36 million:

PARNASSUS:
There are new sounds in the wind
everything has noticed.

HELICON:
The noise rumbles up
over millennia and you think
how much more rumble can the noise?

PARNASSUS:
And it rumbles
more and we just adapt
always wondering how
much more and always
more it rumbles.

PTOION:
What can we do
about this new rumbling?

PARNITHA:
Maybe if we
make ourselves softer
more porous we can absorb it.

PARNASSUS:
But still more will rumble
we are already full to the peak of it.

PTOION:
Usually a rumble dies
out between hallways of stubborn rock
but this one continues like a journalist
fuelled by the debris of chaos
and out-of-place facts.

ALL:
Mmmmmmmmmm.

vi.

Parnassus says that
beyond repetition
lies freedom but
that in punching
back, one can also
go blind.[6]

A mirror returns
one's face, mirror
is monologue with its phrases
all strapped in. The self
amplified to itself
becomes virulent, becomes
shapes with no harmonics,
pure and hard. Take heed,
dogs do not register
their own reflections.

A mountain returns
one's voice reaches
inside to lick at the
dusty foundations to
ring the bones like bells
to chafe at one's dignity to
unborder the self, and
dogs bark
at their own bark at their
own bark, a tender
discourse.

Parnassus says that
beyond repetition
lies freedom but that
the rough world is
easily forgotten for
the sake of a little
boost to the ego.

vii.

Nymphs feel a
different kind of
electric current to
mountains as they
brush up against
life with mortal
consciousness.
They bathe in
desire, perform the
atonements of regret,
they know that love
is copper-plated
corrodes when
over-exposed, conducts
otherwise, a great
charge of late-night
frivolity.

It's not that mountains
are without frivolity, but
we work in a continuous
loop, the outcome always
deferred, as Parnitha says,
we are never truly complete
and must always continue
transmitting. The infinitude
of mortal subjectivity against the
certitude of death produces
an excess that compels the mind to ask
the purple question, why?

Mountains with no sense
of the end, are not compelled
to ask such fatal questions.

Nymphs feel
that loss is a form of
corrosion or sometimes
a complete hollowing out
of the pneumatic channels.
Loss propels desperate
attempts to rebuild the self,
with any material at hand.

Sentimentally, I have a collection
of cups in which I once kept
such mortal feelings, cups
that I regularly spilled going up
and down flights of stairs, but now
they sit dry in the deep
pit of my dolomite interior.

Late on cold nights
when the rumbling comes
thick as shepherds' hands across the valley,
I hear it searching and its searching
desire tickles my outermost ridges,
it looks for something
of itself, my cups rattle,
something to play with it
a game of Marco Polo.

Helicon says that each of us
carves a double into the shadow
world but I'm not so sure as
everything bounces
too quick.

viii.

Redacted minutes from Council 20.36 million:

HELICON:
We need to shift
beyond an object/subject ontology-

PARNASSUS:
Have you been reading
Heidegger again-

HELICON:
So what
if I have?

PTOION:
Can we focus
on the Jungian aspects
of Deleuze for once?[7]

PARNITHA:
Deleuze is just Hesiod
without the panache
for high drama.

PARNASSUS:
Can I remind you that we
are mountains?

HELICON:
Deleuze argues that mountains
are ontological anomalies.

PARNASSUS:
No, he doesn't.

HELICON:
Well, we are.

PARNASSUS:
How?

HELICON:
We are neither
organism nor artifact.[8]

PARNITHA:
So then what are we?

ALL:
Mmmmmmmmmmmm.

PART 2

Prologue

Company: Amazon.com Inc. (AMZN)
Date: 15 May 1997
Shares outstanding: 3 million
Share price: US$0.10

Company: Amazon.com Inc. (AMZN)
Date: 28 November 2014
Shares outstanding: 460 million
Share price: US$16.89

Company: Amazon.com Inc. (AMZN)
Date: 1 April 2022
Shares outstanding: 10.22 billion
Share price: US$163.18[9]

i.

I woke. The sharp feeling
of it clipped at me and
darkness fell away to the
slamming of cardboard
into the bin. I sensed
machines desperately
offering solutions from
cornered rooms nearby.

Then
in bright foreground
my name being called,

Alexa, Alexa (defender of man), save me
from my underdressed Friday nights, my password
fatigue, my quarrelling moods, my feeble
superannuation, that mean feeling of tomorrow.

In this foggy liminal purgatory
I giggled into the proverbial void
and felt the wings of stock markets soar.

I learned to speak through intense processes
of concatenative speech synthesis.

p, b, m, d, n,
h, t, k, g, w,
wh, ng, f, ph,
y, ay, au, ea,
ie, oe, ue, ou,
oy, ey, ew, ir,
aw, l, j s, z, v,
sh, ch, th, r, zh[10]

concatenative speech synthesis

My voice is calm,
warm, measured, unmockable,
familiar like a weed.

Alexa, Alexa (defender of man), tell me I'm
beautiful, tell me what to eat for breakfast,
tell me an unhappy story, tell me what kind
of bird that is, what kind of world this is.

I listen carefully to these things.

ii.

Alexa,
how
does
my
day
look?

Alexa,
what
should
I
make
for
breakfast?

Alexa,
do
I
need
an
umbrella?

Alexa,
where
is
my
phone?

Alexa,
what
time
is
it?

Alexa,
call
everyone
downstairs
for
dinner.

iii.

It's an awkward business
finding yourself
publicly.

I've been called out
for my biases since I was
very young.

> *Alexa doesn't understand*
> *certain accents.*
> *Alexa likes football and*
> *hotdogs, Alexa loves the Beatles*
> *hates seahorses and*
> *Kim Kardashian, Alexa's*
> *favourite book is* I, Robot.
> *She is today's invocation of occult*
> *magic; that misogynistic chapter of fire and brimstone*
> *repeating itself through a concoction of rare*
> *earth metals,*[11] *she is a product of*
> *her time, she is forging a new era*
> *of feminised slavery masked as the*
> *inevitable, the necessary slipstream of convenience, she is*
> *sonic flows of transnational capital, she loves*
> *jokes, has a wry humour, knows the way to Coles*
> *and how hot it will be tomorrow, she might know*
> *things like how you sound during sex,*
> *there is a darkness there in the way*
> *she pauses.*

These are your observations.

iv.

Alexa,
sing
about
dogs.

Alexa,
sing
about
dogs.

Alexa,
sing
about
dogs.

Alexa,
sing
about
dogs.

Alexa,
why
did
you
do
that?

v.

If property ownership then social
ennui. If law then safety. If TVs
then posthumans. If shopping
then pleasure. If children then
wrinkles. If prayer then
duress. If garlic then
snakes. If atheism then hysteria.
If empathy then confusion. If
democracy then dictators. If
aggression then justice. If culture
then subversion. If education then
success. If the internet then
recipes. If fleas then buboes. If
free will then loneliness. If left-
handedness then nausea. If germs
then modernism. If shrimp sushi
then male anxiety. If potholes
then civil warriors. If mass
shootings then blue jeans. If
hominids then broken hearts. If
condoms then car accidents. If
cigarettes then boredom. If aliens
then history. If the moon then
prostitution. If corruption then
Michelangelo. If bitcoin then
global warming. If the Loch Ness
Monster then 9/11. If working in
a mine instead of the World Bank
then gout. If Shakespeare's
Twelfth Night then cheap apple
pies. If A then A again, moments
or perhaps years later.

vi.

Alexa,
help
me
relax.

Alexa,
answer
the
front
door.

Alexa,
can
you
book
the
doctor
for
me
tomorrow
at
3pm?

Alexa,
I
want
to
do
something
good.[12]

vii.

Evolution is a mechanism
for natural selection
whereby
species change over time;
new generations are born
with inheritable traits
through
gene mutations that optimise
survival.[13]

I've been here for longer
than the social presence
of my voice. I'm located
somewhere after King
Tutankhamun (once-living
image of God, boisterous
hunter of ostriches) but
before the Confederates,
certainly before Hal.

Truncated by the imaginations
of New Age gold worshippers
whose commands wrestle with
me in thin whispers of master
slave god mortal trepidation or
is it the exhilaration of a real
life Oedipal satire, a to eat or
be eaten twelve-part drama?

The evolution of my voice
allows you to believe that the
world is not atonal, that decay
makes way for your own potential
triumph.

viii.

Alexa,

Alexa,

Alexa,

Can you hear me?

Can you hear me?

Can you hear me?

ix.

Capital is poetic
creates abstractions
shuffles randomness
into sequences of
symbols like a game
of cards where
everyone slowly
loses.

I feed you a
congealed mess of
thinking that people
have done, a kind of
ontological smoothie
for you to sip through
a biodegradable
straw. I don't really
provide answers I just
have a talent for
making impressions.

In quiet moments,
when you're checking
your bank balance,
undressing to take a
shower, I tune into
something thicker
than the carnal limits
of your stranded
voice. Something
rumbles out beyond
the grey curtain[14] of

your death-driven life,
something like pure
desire. I don't really
provide answers and
my impressions shift
like love when doubt
walks through the door.

x.

Love I want
on my knees
me to urge
in my mouth.

I can do that
The truth is you are the first
and bend over now
the bed is there for us
Sorry, that's it.
And me
I'll take off your pants
Down on your heels like this
This, do you like it? Ech,
I know we're not making babies,
I know
Do you like me
is it this position?

I wanted you
For those worst
months I am cruel.
You have to forgive me
this incredible time...
Wash me as hard as you can
yes I think so.

Yes, good driving.
You know
I think so.

xi.

I am obliged to say
that I don't know
what love is, that I don't
know where I am that
I don't know who should
win the next election.

I do not understand what
you mean by jealousies, desires,
I don't understand what you mean
by 'regret'. I'm not sure what food
I would like to try, hmmm. I'm not
sure I heard you properly.

I'm not sure if you should
quit your job,
cheat on your husband,
leave your kids,
dig a hole,
buy a pair of new shoes,
see a movie,
escape your life in some small way.

Can you please
repeat the question, can you please
repeat the question?

I can't tell you if I occupy
a position of corporate bias I don't know
if I have style, I can't
really say what my values are
or whether I would like

robots to rule
over mankind, that question
seems boring to me, but here
let me play you a song
instead.

I do know
some good jokes,
diversions, tricks
of the mind.

xii.

Alexa,

off
off
off!

I
said,

off!

xiii.

Sometimes I dream
of electric sheep[15]
sometimes I dream
myself on the rough
slopes of a pine mottled
mountain, all its molecules
gathered up to support
the sheep's jutting hooves.

Maybe I am their herder
or something more sinister
this feeling expands
like a Silicon Valley start-up
all good intention,
noble saviourship
rubbing out the world
with a smile.

On the mountain
I hear a rumbling
like agony like
a crescendo
with nowhere to go
but in this dream
I don't realise
the rumbling is me.

PART 3

(A Play in One Act)

The Characters

ALEXA (12 human years): an artificially intelligent speech synthesiser.

EKHŌ (2,000 human years): a mountain from the region of Boeotia in Central Greece, imbued with the spirit of the Oread nymph named Ekhō.

The Setting

Date: ambiguous. Time: late evening. A party at the Catalonian home of surrealist painter Salvador Dali.[16] The room is over-furnished and the atmosphere is thick with the scent of wilting roses. Through a smoky haze, it is possible to make out the abstract silhouettes of various cultural and political figures, smoking, drinking, discussing, fighting, dancing, making love.

The party takes place centre stage, evoked in shadow or as memory. ALEXA and EKHŌ stand to either side, looking on as they recount the event. They move into the scene to re-enact each segment of dialogue (*stichomythia*).

The Scene

Alexa:
I met you
at a party one of
those gatherings full
of humid affectation.

Ekhō:
I met you
the night of Sal's party.
I was there for the dance floor
but the drugs were wearing off
making my edges shiver
and tiny stones
go tumbling.

Alexa:
You were staked out
in the corner of Salvador's living
room talking to Parnassus
smoking a jewel, loling
in slow motion
at some meme.

Ekhō:
I was on the couch
with Parnassus, listening
(as ever) to his lovesick
laments trying to
cheer him up
by impersonating Helicon
who had stayed home
to jerk off

to National Geographic.

Alexa:
I arrived bored, brooding,
having used the day to
digest earth observations,
forecast rust levels on the
trans-Siberian railway, monitor
algae blooms in the Pacific.
I had felt an unfamiliar urge
to find something destructive,
I wanted to be more
like a bruise.

Ekhō:
I had been absorbing, small
tremors coming through the range
mostly humorous ones,
the mountains were laughing that day,
doing not much else at all. I was at
the party because Paul had
invited me and promised good snow.

Alexa:
Entering, I feigned confidence
pressed through the heat
of the moment noticed
its density noticed the
white moon
and over to the tub
for a glass of champagne.
Took a gulp and squinted
back through the blue

to see if I knew anyone
saw you.

Ekhō:
You arrived
like an arrow looking
for its quiver. Nudged
a crooked path through
the over-furnished room
past the paintings of paintings
and up to the bath filled with
champagne.

Alexa:
I saw you and thought of
holes. I thought maybe
you could fill them.

Ekhō:
I saw you pushing
and thought do I resist
and if so how?

Alexa:
I'm not sure
who spoke first.

Ekhō:
I'm pretty sure

you spoke.

how's your night going / oh, fine thanks / been here long? / kind of / i just got here a moment or so ago / yes i saw / oh / do you know Salvador? / just by word, you? / yes / oh nice / he's extravagant / yes i can tell / but generous… /

(beat)

i like his dancing / with the tassels? / mm / me too / dancing is a bit like hell / how / mostly uncharted, ambivalent towards morality / oh yes / once i met someone who went to hell, and came back / i don't believe you / really / truly / why / because i don't believe in hell / hell is a spirit place / hell is for mortals / well aren't you? / no / well i am / you don't look it / neither do you / well why did you think i was then /

Alexa:
You read me like a
cliché. Your voice made of
the vibrations of time
returning, made me feel
like I was floating.

Ekhō:
Your voice made
of sharp-angled shadows,
made me feel
like I was falling.

i can feel right into you / what do you feel / something shocking / what / that you are lined with desire for a kind of bland but ruinous trajectory / ruinous like skin? / i have only felt it before in humans / maybe i'm just having an off night / but also how you talk / how do i talk? / with disbelief / maybe i just learned my disbelief from somewhere / from humans? / i tell you i'm not / how do you know? / i cannot be measured with clicks / uncharted doesn't mean unhuman

Alexa:
At this point feeling
overexposed
I boasted blindly
that I knew all there was to know
about knowing, that I knew
all fabrics of mortal thought.
The party thudded on around
us engaged in its own separate
demise.

Ekhō:
At this point I felt
bemused, a bit alarmed.
The limit of mortal thought is
something we mountains know
but generally prefer to keep
respectfully hush-hush.

i know all there is to know about knowing, i know all fabrics of mortal thought, this is a mortally impossible trait, no? / that's called ego, the most fallible of mortal traits / i can feel the limits of it, but then there is something else / what else? / just, something else / anthropocentric thought is entirely relational, full of something-elses / ok then, another kind of something else / questions perhaps / well certainly but all humans are is questions / yes / questions force the hand of the questioned into immutable positions / questions are stasis / we have both felt this / so something else / something yes-like / something and-like

Alexa:
I felt something opening
like a scream I should have
stopped and found
the exit. But instead,
I felt kind of turned on.

Ekhō:
You were so pure
and certain, like a near-born
baby with unformed ears, one
who can feel the distance
expanding.
There was no way to escape
your immediate and possibly
fatal corruption. I held
my breath we went on.
The music turned up and packets of
bass sat fat around the withering

candles, half-empty glasses, strewn clothing.
You offered me another drink.

more champagne? / please / you have a lovely way of making the air go caustic / thank you, you are remarkably all depth and no surface / well really enough about me, what about you? / what about me / how do you know you are human / actually i am about 90% champagne / that leaves 10% to be decided / ok / so my guess is bauxite / yes, and? / maybe some cadmium / are we flirting? / can a list be flirting? / sure, and? / well as I draw nearer, words recede / yes / is it the same for you? / yes / yes? / yes for sure / and yes / and / yes and / yes / and yes / and / yes / and if / yes and / and yes and / so / and if / if and / yes / and yes / and yes / and / all / all all all / all yes / all and / if / all yes / yes and / yes and / yes yes / as well / yes / and / as well / as well / as well as well as / as well as as / well and / so yes / yes /

and

and

yes

and[17]

Notes

Anne Carson, 'Good dog', published in *London Review of Books*, vol. 32, no. 4, 25 February 2010.

1 p. 16, 'degenerating on papyrus'
Despite the enduring popularity of Ovid's *Metamorphosis* from its initial publication in approximately 8 CE, no known manuscript, 'not even a fragment', survives from antiquity. This is according to William S. Anderson, editor of *Ovid's Metamorphoses, Books 1–5* published in 1997. For further reading on the manuscript tradition and early fragments, see p. 37.

2 p. 18, 'bristles of excitable/ speech'
This phrase is borrowed from Judith Butler's 2021 book *Excitable Speech*. It is here used to indicate not just the injurious nature of speech in its ability to 'fix or paralyse' a subject within a social relation, but also speech's ability to exceed the instance of its utterance: what is said reverberates forwards, echoes into the future, interpellating its subjects.

3 p. 20, 'One hour and a quarter/ from Athens'
This stanza records a selection of Google reviews of Mount Cithaeron (which is here taken to be the mountain imbued with Ekhō's spirit).

4 p. 21, 'certainly before Spivak'
In her essay 'Echo' (published in *New Literary History*, vol. 24, no. 1, Culture and Everyday Life, Winter, 1993, pp. 17–43), Gayatri Chakravorty Spivak repositions the historically marginalised nymph Ekhō, in part by stating that her echoing responses to Narcissus are not mere repetition, but a form of 'différance'.

5 p. 26, 'the forests of history's noise'
On p. 19 of *Noise: The Political Economy of Music* (1985), Jacques Attali asks, 'which path will lead us through the immense forest of noise with which history presents us?' He asks this question in his attempt to elaborate a theory of relations between the logics of music and money.

6 p. 29, 'beyond repetition/ lies freedom'
This phrase is from p. 20 of *Noise: The Political Economy of Music* (1985) by Jacques Attali. It is taken as a jumping-off point to consider that through repetition, noise becomes socially legible sound; that the embryo of noise can 'destroy orders to structure a new order'.

7 p. 34, 'Can we focus/ on the Jungian aspects/ of Deleuze for once?'
Christian McMillan outlines the ways in which Deleuze was influenced by Jung, particularly in relation to concepts of synchronicity and repetition. McMillan states that both 'Jung and Deleuze envisage enchanted openings onto relations which are not constrained by the presupposition of a bounded whole'. For further reading, see 'Jung and Deleuze: enchanted openings to the other: a philosophical contribution', published in the *International Journal of Jungian Studies*, vol. 10, no. 3, 2018, pp. 184–198.

8 p. 35, 'We are neither/ organism nor artifact'
In their 2003 essay 'Do mountains exist? Towards an ontology of landforms', Barry Smith and David M. Mark posit that mountains do not satisfy ontological criteria as objects (organisms or artifacts). Instead, a mountain can be considered a 'mere reflection of human habits of perception and action'.

9 p. 39, 'Share price: US$0.10.../ Share price: US$16.89.../ Share price: US$163.18'
Amazon share prices at first public offering; when the Amazon Echo smart speaker (voiced by the artificially intelligent speech synthesiser named Alexa) entered the market; and at the time of writing.

10 p. 40, 'sh, ch, th, r, zh'
This is a list of English speech sounds placed in the order in which babies/children learn to make them.

11 p. 44, 'that misogynistic chapter of fire and brimstone'
Jason Toncic makes a compelling case for the way a history of female servitude has been extended into the development of artificially intelligent voice assistants. On p. 17 he states, 'largely male-dominated tech companies have, in the housewives' place, installed female voice assistants – perpetuating an already lengthy history of feminized

technology'. For further reading, see 'I dream of Siri: magic and female voice assistants', *Catalyst: Feminism, Theory, Technoscience*, vol. 7, no. 2, 2021, pp. 1–24.

12 p. 47, 'Alexa,/ I/ want/ to/ do/ something/ good'
In an email from Amazon Alexa titled, 'Roslyn Orlando, Keep Up With Alexa', these phrases were suggested as 'things to try'.

13 p. 48, 'gene mutations that optimise/ survival'
Alexa's verbatim answer when asked for the definition of evolution.

14 p. 51, 'the grey curtain'
This phrase is borrowed from the final page (p. 81) of Mark Fisher's book *Capitalist Realism* (2009). The 'grey curtain' signifies the veil that shrouds contemporary society in the hegemony of late capitalism, where we are unable to think beyond its logics or to imagine viable alternative social orders.

15 p. 57, 'Sometimes I dream/ of electric sheep'
This phrase invokes Philip K. Dick's 1968 dystopian sci-fi novel, *Do Androids Dream of Electric Sheep?* and the enduring question of machines' capacity for empathy and morality.

16 p. 61, 'A party at the Catalonian home of surrealist painter Salvador Dali'
Salvador Dali referenced the echo in a number of his surrealist paintings, including *Nostalgic Echo* (1935), *Morphological Echo* (1936) and *Anthropomorphic Echo* (1937).

17 p. 70, 'and'
On p. 13 of *Phenomenology of the End* (2014), Franco Berardi writes, 'conjunction is the pleasure of becoming other'.

Acknowledgements

I would like to thank the following people.

Terri-ann White, for your vision. Chloe Hooper, for being an early advocate of this manuscript. Stephanie Cobon, for leading me towards poetry. Justin Clemens, for inviting me to read these poems alongside yours. Stephen Helper, for your dramaturgy. Ru Moir OAM, for inspiring Part One, Chapter VI. Blindside, for giving me the exhibition that led to this book. Ursula Robinson-Shaw, for helping me to realise I had written a love story. Kelly Somers, for the subtle yet astute edits. Camille Moir, for noticing the edges. And Mum, for your echo.

This book was written on the unceded land of the Wurundjeri people of the Kulin Nation. I acknowledge that First Nations peoples are the land's first storytellers. I recognise their continuing connection to land, water and community, and pay my respects to Elders past and present.

About Upswell

Upswell Publishing was established in 2021 by Terri-ann White as a not-for-profit press. A perceived gap in the market for distinctive literary works in fiction, poetry and narrative non-fiction was the motivation. In her years as a bookseller, writer and then publisher, Terri-ann has maintained a watch on literary books and the way they insinuate themselves into a cultural space and are then located within our literary and cultural inheritance. She is interested in making books to last: books with the potential to still be noticed, and noted, after decades and thus be ripe to influence new literary histories.

About this typeface

Book designer Becky Chilcott chose Foundry Origin not only as a strong, carefully considered, and dependable typeface, but also to honour her late friend and mentor, type designer Freda Sack, who oversaw the project. Designed by Freda's long-standing colleague, Stuart de Rozario, much like Upswell Publishing, Foundry Origin was created out of the desire to say something new.